From 1.30 am on Tuesday January 1st 2002, Irish currency will start to be withdrawn from circulation.

At midnight on Saturday February 9th, it will cease to exist.

From 1.30 am on Tuesday January 1st 2002, Irish currency will start to be withdrawn from circulation.

At midnight on Saturday February 9th, it will cease to exist.

For many years the one pound jar has been the measure for making, buying and selling jam and jelly.

For thirty years the punt or pound has been the largest coin in the Irish currency.

An empty one pound jar weighs 7⅞ oz or 225 g

For many years the one pound jar has been the measure for making, buying and selling jam and jelly.

For thirty years the punt or pound has been the largest coin in the Irish currency.

An empty one pound jar weighs 7⅞ oz or 225 g

20P
50P

5p

2P
5P
1P
10P

In the full one pound jar
the number of one pound
coins was 163

The weight of one pound
coins in the one pound jar
was 4 lb 1¼ oz
or 1 kg 850 g

The total amount of one
pound coins in the one
pound jar was £ 163

In the full one pound jar
the number of one pound
coins was 163

The weight of one pound
coins in the one pound jar
was 4 lb 1¼ oz
or 1 kg 850 g

The total amount of one
pound coins in the one
pound jar was £ 163

In the full one pound jar
the number of 50p coins
was 134

The weight of 50p coins
in the one pound jar
was 4 lb 7⅜ oz
or 2 kg 25 g

The total amount of 50p
coins in the one pound jar
was £ 67

In the full one pound jar
the number of 50p coins
was 134

The weight of 50p coins
in the one pound jar
was 4 lb 7 3/8 oz
or 2 kg 25 g

The total amount of 50p
coins in the one pound jar
was £ 67

20p

In the full one pound jar
the number of 20p coins
was 206

The weight of 20p coins
in the one pound jar
was 4 lb 5 oz
or 1 kg 955 g

The total amount of 20p
coins in the one pound jar
was £ 41.20 p

In the full one pound jar
the number of 20p coins
was 206

The weight of 20p coins
in the one pound jar
was 4 lb 5 oz
or 1 kg 955 g

The total amount of 20p
coins in the one pound jar
was £ 41.20 p

In the full one pound jar
the number of 10p coins
was 322

The weight of 10p coins
in the one pound jar
was 4 lb 5½ oz
or 1 kg 970 g

The total amount of 10p
coins in the one pound jar
was £ 32.20 p

In the full one pound jar
the number of 10p coins
was 322

The weight of 10p coins
in the one pound jar
was 4 lb 5½ oz
or 1 kg 970 g

The total amount of 10p
coins in the one pound jar
was £ 32.20 p

10P

In the full one pound jar
the number of 5p coins
was 528

The weight of 5p coins
in the one pound jar
was 4 lb $4\frac{3}{8}$ oz
or 1 kg 940 g

The total amount of 5p
coins in the one pound jar
was £ 26.40 p

In the full one pound jar
the number of 5p coins
was 528

The weight of 5p coins
in the one pound jar
was 4 lb 4⅜ oz
or 1 kg 940 g

The total amount of 5p
coins in the one pound jar
was £ 26.40 p

In the full one pound jar
the number of 2p coins
was 210

The weight of 2p coins
in the one pound jar
was 3 lb 12⅝ oz
or 1 kg 720 g

The total amount of 2p
coins in the one pound jar
was £ 4.20 p

In the full one pound jar
the number of 2p coins
was 210

The weight of 2p coins
in the one pound jar
was 3 lb 12⅝ oz
or 1 kg 720 g

The total amount of 2p
coins in the one pound jar
was £ 4.20 p

In the full one pound jar
the number of 1p coins
was 408

The weight of 1p coins
in the one pound jar
was 3 lb 10 3/8 oz
or 1 kg 655 g

The total amount of 1p
coins in the one pound jar
was £ 4.08 p

In the full one pound jar
the number of 1p coins
was 408

The weight of 1p coins
in the one pound jar
was 3 lb 10⅜ oz
or 1 kg 655 g

The total amount of 1p
coins in the one pound jar
was £ 4.08 p

In seven full one pound jars
the total number of coins
was 1971

In seven full one pound jars
the total weight of coins
was 28 lb 14 5/8 oz
or 13 kg 11 g

In seven full one pound jars
the total amount of coins
was £ 338.08 p

In seven full one pound jars
the total number of coins
was 1971

In seven full one pound jars
the total weight of coins
was 28 lb 14⅝ oz
or 13 kg 11 g

In seven full one pound jars
the total amount of coins
was £ 338.08 p